CITYHOPPERS

CITYHOPPERS
SHORT-HAUL AIRLINERS AT WORK

Philip Handleman

Airlife
England

First published in the UK in 1998
by Airlife Publishing Ltd

British Library Cataloguing-in-Publication Data
  A Catalogue record for this book
  is available from the British Library

ISBN 1 85310 895 2

Typeset by Phoenix Typesetting, Ilkley, West Yorkshire.
Printed in Singapore

Airlife Publishing Ltd
101 Longden Road, Shrewsbury, SY3 9EB, England

Dedication

To my wife, Mary.

The Author

Since his first flight in a Piper Cub at 12 years of age, Philip Handleman has ardently pursued his interest in airplanes and flying. He has been a licensed pilot for more than 26 years, and currently owns and flies two restored aircraft of military lineage, including an open-cockpit Stearman biplane.

The author of 10 previous aviation books and many dozens of aviation articles, Handleman is a recognized aviation authority. For many years he has beautifully captured a wide range of airplanes in his still photography. His honors include having one of his photographs of the Thunderbirds air demonstration team selected as the image for the 1997 U.S. postage stamp commemorating the 50th anniversary of the U.S. Air Force as a separate military service.

In addition, Handleman is president of Handleman Filmworks, an award-winning television production company that has produced highly acclaimed documentaries. He and his wife, Mary, divide their time between their home in Birmingham, Michigan and a private airstrip in the nearby countryside.

Acknowledgements

The following individuals and organisations assisted in the preparation of this book. Without their help, the project would have foundered. I am grateful for their co-operation.

Michelle R. King, Continental Express
Shirley Sloan, Marketing, American Eagle
Tim Kincaid, Corporate Communications, AMR Eagle, Inc.
Jonathan Hinkles, Commercial Executive, City Flyer Express
Mary Smith, Public Relations Officer, Commercial Airways (Pty) Limited
Cimber Air
Cristina Silvestri, Corporate Communication, Air Dolomiti
Nicola Watkins, CityJet
Simone Spilker, Assistant Manager of Public Relations, Eurowings
Manx Airlines
Christian Dahl, Sales and Marketing, British Airways Express
Sheena Harrison, Public Relations Co-ordinator, Air UK Limited
Lyn Taylor, Publicity Department, British World Airlines Ltd
Avro International Aerospace
Pat Zerbe, Manager of Public Relations, Raytheon Aircraft Company
Mary Catherine Johnson, Vice-President of Corporate Communications, Gulfstream International Airlines
Gaby Leyba, Customer Service Lead, Gulfstream International Airlines
Art Skelly, Director of Airports, Monroe County, Florida
Eugene Garcia, Captain of Fire Department, Key West International Airport
Bill Jones, Vice-President of Operations, Pan Am Air Bridge
Viola Cole, Reservations/Marketing, Mountain West Airlines
Sarah Pitcher, Vice-President of Corporate Communications, Mesa Air Group
Jeffrey Coons, Director of Passenger Services, Skyway Airlines
Astral Aviation, Inc.
Midwest Express Airlines
A. Panarese, Communication Department, Aero International (Regional)
Lesley Shepherd, Secretary to External Relations Manager, European Regional Airlines Association
Benet J. Wilson, Director of Public Relations, Regional Airline Association

Diane Douglas, Manager of Public Relations, Skywest Airlines
Air Canada
Sofia Katsidou, Press and Public Relations, Lufthansa CityLine
Claudia Schreiber, Lufthansa CityLine
Tyrolean Airways
Anita Paalanen, Public Relations, Bombardier Regional Aircraft
Construcciones Aeronauticas, S.A.
Arkia Israeli Airlines Ltd
Dennis Erickson, Manager of Corporate Communications, Canadian Regional Airlines
Leanne Perreault, Manager of Sales Planning and Corporate Communications, Air Ontario
Augsburg Airways
Marie-Claire Ward, Commercial Executive, Brymon Airways
Sonja Hentsch, Marketing, Fairchild Dornier
Sylvia Saenz, Marketing Administration, Fairchild Dornier
Heather Orr, Communications Specialist, US Airways
Air Engiadina
Marilda Bastos, Public Relations, Empresa Brasileira de Aeronautica S.A.
Air Exel Commuter
Lilia Polin, Corporate Identity Department, Delta Air Lines
Ria van Oeveren, Communication Department, Fokker Aviation
Olympic Aviation S.A.
Pekka Valimaki, Managing Director, Karair
Ole Pedersen, President, SAS Commuter
Vlaamse Luchttransport Maatschappij N.V.
Koninklijke Luchtvaart Maatschappij N.V.
Sharon D. Guest, Executive Assistant – Marketing, Chicago Express Airlines
Express Airlines
Mesaba Aviation, Inc.
Cristina Rahm, Saab Aircraft AB, Saab-Scania
Regional Airlines
Air Ostrava
Skyways
Sandra Trautmann, Public Relations Manager, Deutsche BA
Manfred Winkler, Corporate Communications, Crossair

Introduction

The Ascent of Commercial Air Travel

Years ago, the prospect of airline travel conjured up images of adventurous journeys and glamorous surroundings. By the late 1930s, airliners had reached a new plateau in reliability with a concomitant level of public confidence. All-metal cabins, cantilevered wings, high-output radial engines, radio navigational gear, and a proliferating infrastructure of airports dotting the landscape signalled air transport's replacement of the old cruise lines and passenger railways.

Whether hop-scotching the Pacific in a clipper or traversing the Appalachians in a mainliner, flying aboard a commercial aircraft had become *de rigueur*, the milieu of the famous and the affluent. Appealing to this ritzy stratum, attempts were made to mimic the luxury of the grand ocean liners and railway coaches.

Sleeping berths and smoking rooms were among the amenities offered on the larger airliners. When the pre-flight was completed, pilots could be seen greeting the boarding passengers. The restaurants at layover points had fresh baked goods awaiting deplaning passengers.

The architecture at the newly-sprouting airports boldly asserted the import of aviation with a fullness of style, at times suggesting a touch of nobility. Certain terminals, like those incorporating art deco design, manifested an elegance. Air travel in the Golden Age of Flight was not devoid of the jostling that comes from flying through weather or of the noise from poorly-insulated cabins, but 'the getting there' was an exciting and welcome part of the time away from home.

While a new-found utilitarianism emerged following World War II, emphasizing efficiency over opulence, commercial air travel still offered a sense of the fantastic. A trip to the airport meant parents and children dressing up to the hilt in their Sunday best. Spare time caused by a mechanical delay was passed delightedly on the observation deck, watching giant four-engine prop jobs roar into the heavens. Steamer trunks brimming to capacity were obligatory for the two-week winter vacation to Florida.

Senior flight crew in this transitional era were the Roscoe Turner types, swashbuckling pioneers and barnstormers nearing the ends of their careers, at last flying something respectable. Some of the old-timers, especially those on international routes, exuded the aura of the legendary sea captains – long beards, stern demeanors, double-breasted uniforms with gold-braided epaulets. Once established at cruise, they would invite you to come and take a look in the cockpit.

The very success of the airlines and their ability to safely and cost-effectively transport incredible numbers of people to an array of destinations on a daily basis brought the magic of air travel to the reach of the ordinary person and, in time, the mystique faded. The attire of choice for commercial flying is now the track suit. Long lines at ticket counters and again at metal detectors reflect a régime more akin to the bus station.

Baggage retrieval often involves an interminable wait in which suitcases are dribbled out onto the conveyor belt one by one. It is incongruous that an airport's air-side accommodates spectacularly advanced technology, allowing pilots to nonchalantly navigate with pin-point accuracy to anywhere in the airspace encompassing the planet, while ground-side in the darkened and low-ceilinged caverns mayhem reigns where paying passengers seek to collect their luggage.

The litany of deficiencies has become second nature to the frequent air traveller: inadequate airport parking, overbooked flights, cramped seating, etc. The congestion in the airspace around major hubs continues to worsen. At the same time, many existing terminals are handling capacities far in excess of their design limits. Yet, few major new airports have been built in the last 20 years. Efforts to expand capacity at established airports, by and large, are occurring late and with all the managerial ineptitude of local politicos.

The corner of the airfield that harbours the short haulers offers a story a little different. Most commuter aircraft, like the old airliners, have propellers, albeit ones driven by turbines. Dwarfed by the jumbos, these regional aircraft, as they are sometimes called, generally require the passengers to venture out into the open air of the ramp to board them.

Once airborne, those seated in the cabin of a commuter airliner know that they are in an aeroplane, contrary to the numbing sensation, experienced in the mid-cabin of a widebody with the blinds drawn and a second-rate feature film being projected on the bulkhead screen. Although far from rekindling the glory days of air travel, the regionals represent real flying.

Regional Airline Operations

In the US, regional air carriers are defined by the Federal Aviation Administration as airlines whose fleets predominantly consist of aircraft with a seating capacity of 60 seats or less. A more general definition would be air carriers serving a particular region with relatively small piston, turboprop, and jet aircraft.

Commuter airlines cater to the short-haul market. In today's hub-and-spoke system, the regionals handle the shorter routes that link large metropolitan areas to smaller outlying communities. Such routes are not as mature as the routes connecting big cities. In many instances, such routes also lack intense competition. Whereas there may be a half dozen airlines operating a dedicated fleet of Boeing 727s or larger aircraft with service from a given snowbound urban centre in the northern US to sunny Miami, there are usually just one or two regionals providing service between that same hub, Miami, and a given outlying community.

Indeed, the average route distance for commuter airlines in the US is 223 miles. Also, in the US, the regionals service 780 airports while the majors service just 252. Of those airports with commuter airline service, 72 per cent have no other regularly-scheduled airline service. European regionals service approximately 340 communities in more than 26 countries. In fact, every 10 seconds a regional airliner takes off or lands in Europe. Clearly, the regionals, both in the US and in Europe, provide a vital link for many communities.

In the US during 1995, the most recent year for which statistics are available, regionals carried nine per cent of all airline passengers. This represented a total of 57.2 million passenger enplanements. European regionals had about 44 million passenger enplanements.

In recent years, the growth of commuter airlines, as measured by revenue passenger miles, has outpaced the increases of the majors. This trend is expected to continue into the foreseeable future.

Consolidation has begun to affect the commuter airline industry just as it has had an impact on the aviation world as a whole. Since 1980, the number of US regionals has shrunk from a total of 214 carriers to a current total of 124. Among the top 50 commuter airlines, 36 had code-sharing relationships with major airlines. These affiliations provide greater visibility for the regionals because travel agents can easily access their flight information via computer reservations systems. The 10 largest regionals account for a massive 75 per cent of the industry's enplanements.

It can be expected that the few remaining majors will seek to gobble-up the more established regionals in markets compatible with their existing route structure. Regional airline operations tend to be concentrated in a geographic area (hence, the term 'regional') so that respective markets are relatively easily defined and measurable with respect to growth factors.

In the wake of deregulation a new phenomenon emerged within the US airline industry. Airlines became the targets of leveraged buy-outs with financiers taking control, many of whom could hardly tell the difference between a throttle lever and a rudder pedal. At the same time, with governmental barriers to market-place entry virtually eliminated, start-ups abounded including those that were predicated on the concoctions of lawyers and travel agents.

With the protection customarily afforded to utilities eliminated, the shaky financial underpinnings of the airlines turned precarious. Once proud industry names went the way of bankruptcy and in some cases vanished altogether. One wonders what the industry's founding fathers, men like Eddie Rickenbacker, Howard Hughes, and Juan Trippe, would make of events since their departure from the scene.

Fortunately, since the disruptions to the petroleum supply of the 1970s, fuel availability and pricing have remained fairly stable. As long as this critical variable continues to be steady and the general economy does not falter, demand for commercial air travel should keep increasing.

However, the primary driver of the commuter airline success in recent years is that same ingredient that has always been at the heart of any airline's good fortune – the indomitable spirit of the flight crews. Woefully underpaid in relation to their enormous responsibilities, it can hardly be said that commuter airline pilots are motivated by monetary reward. Surely, these aviators have the prospect of accumulating flight hours and moving up to the majors where the pecuniary benefits are better, but still logic dictates that they are sustained by a love of flying.

As things now stand, the regionals serve as a kind of farm league for the majors where young, aspiring pilots can do their appenticeships. Increasingly, these pilots are being indoctrinated into the world of airline flying through comprehensive *ab initio* training programs. Typically, substantial flight simulator-time is a part of the instruction syllabus such that the pilots are exposed to a wide range of scenarios, including emergency situations, that would otherwise come only by means of many years of flying experience. The result is more rounded and 'savvy' aviators.

Commuter Aircraft

Commuter airliners are getting larger and more sophisticated. These changes have been prompted in large measure by consumer preferences and safety considerations.

Following some highly publicised commuter accidents, the Federal Aviation Administration mandated in 1995 that from March 1997 aircraft in scheduled service with 10 to 30 seats would no longer be governed by Part 135 of the Federal Aviation Regulations, but instead would be covered by the more stringent Part 121 that had previously only applied to aircraft in scheduled service with more than 30 seats. Essentially, this regulatory change required that the same rules pertaining to the majors with regard to training, aircraft certification, and operating requirements also apply to commuter aircraft. The American commuter airline industry supported this change.

The average number of seats on a US commuter airliner is 24.6, and the trend is towards increasing the seating capacity. Not only are the individual aircraft produced for the regional fleet growing in physical size, the aggregate number of aircraft in the fleet is growing. US regional air carriers operated a total of 2,138 aircraft, and in the next decade are projected to have 3,250 aircraft in use. European regionals are currently operating 670 aircraft with similar

It is unlikely that airliners in the future will be built as free-standing, one-of-a-kind types. Rather, airliners will most likely belong to a 'family' of aircraft sharing a general configuration and certain components. More market sectors may be served with the manufacturer offering a range of aircraft. This approach to airliner-building should, in the long term, allow the manufacturer to spread developmental costs over several similar products and to achieve economies of scale. Reflective of this emerging phenomenon among regional airliner makers is this formation-flight of various versions of the Avro Regional Jet, which the company has labelled 'The Regional Jetliner.'

prospects for growth in the overall fleet.

The benefits of advanced technology are increasingly apparent in the products available to the regional airline markets. Some of the new commuter airliners have 'glass cockpits' with the latest in electronic digital flight control systems, GPS (Global Positioning System) navigational units, moving map displays, etc.

The long-standing advantages of the turboprop over the jet, which include fuel efficiency and short-field capability, account for the preponderance of turboprop-powered aircraft in the commuter airline fleet. As this performance gap decreases between turboprop and jet due, in part, to technical strides in jet engine technology and as the flying public becomes more demanding, there is expected to be a move towards increased acquisition of jets for the commuter fleet. Indeed, several commuter airliner manufacturers are in the process of introducing twin jets to complement their existing turboprop offerings. Additionally, a hybrid using tilt-rotor technology is in the offing.

Commuter aircraft manufacturing is a global industry, and unlike the production of major airliners which is dominated by the two giant companies, Boeing and Airbus, no oligarchy yet exists in the making of commuter airliners.

Countries in various corners of the world have encouraged an indigenous capacity for the design and assembly of commuter airliners. Such aircraft are perceived as less demanding technically and financially than the development and production of major airliners. The payback can be meaningful in terms of the populace enjoying skilled job opportunities and the foreign trade balance benefiting from a marketable export product. There is also the intangibility of national pride associated with a home-borne product that bears technological sophistication and that engages in high-visibility usage worldwide.

The most common commuter airliner in US service is the Beechcraft 1900 with 265 units in operation. However, the Saab 340 accounts for the largest share, nearly 14 per cent, of the seating capacity of US regionals. The EMBRAER EMB-120 is a close second with a 12.5 per cent penetration. Indicative of the international character of the industry is the fact that more than 75 per cent of commuter airliners are built in European nations.

With increasing aircraft size and sophistication, the dynamics of the industry are in a state of flux. Regional aircraft are looking more and more like their big brothers. The very elements that made the production of commuter airliners possible by secondary players that were beyond the reach of major airliners have begun to shift. Accordingly, undertaking a commuter airliner programme from scratch involves a far greater capital investment than before.

The trend that is occurring among the regional airlines is taking hold among the manufacturers as well. That is to say, consolidation in the ranks of the commuter aircraft manufacturers has started. A leading European example is the recent affiliation of ATR (itself an international consortium), Avro, and Jetstream under the banner of Aero International (Regional) or AI(R). On a trans-Atlantic scale, there is the even newer combination of Fairchild and Dornier. These sorts of alliances can be expected to continue, and perhaps some aerospace giants will seize the chance to establish themselves in this niche market by acquiring makers of regional aircraft.

(Opposite Above):
Consumer demand for commuter aircraft with cutting-edge characteristics has prompted manufacturers to respond, in part, with designs resembling downsized versions of the major jetliners. Faster cruise speeds and the ability to overfly a lot of bad weather come with jet-powered aircraft. Strides in power-plant technology have resulted in jet engines with higher thrust that can operate more fuel-efficiently. At the same time, progress in propulsive systems has combined with improvements in structures to facilitate better short-field performance for jet aircraft. Accordingly, newer purpose-built jets are replacing turbo-props on an increasing number of regional routes. Soon the EMBRAER EMB-145, a twin-jet in the 50-seat class, will enter commercial service as a commuter airliner.

(Opposite Below):
Until fairly recently there had tended to be a technology gap between regional and major airliners. That chasm, however, is quickly narrowing as advancements in avionics, propulsion, materials, and manufacturing processes make sophistication on the commuter level more affordable and cost effective. The new SAAB 2000 twin-turbo-prop, for example, features a state-of-the-art instrument panel where vital flight data are drawn up on six CRT displays.

ATR 42

In early 1996, three aircraft-manufacturing companies representing operations in France, Italy, and the United Kingdom formed a joint venture called Aero International (Regional) and was known by the simple acronym of AI(R). The two commuter airliner units of British Aerospace, namely Avro International and Jetstream, linked up with Avions de Transport Régional (ATR), which itself is a consortium between Alenia and Aérospatiale. Main product lines include several versions of the ATR, the Avro RJ, and the Jetstream. Having hubs in Houston, Newark, and Cleveland, Continental Express, a wholly-owned subsidiary of Continental Airlines, serves over four million passengers each year. The parent company traces its lineage back to the well-known Varney Speed Lines, which began operations in 1934 with a route connecting the border town of El Paso, Texas with Pueblo, Colorado. This ATR 42 is representative of the 37 currently operated by Continental Express.

(Above):
The ATR 42-300 is powered by Pratt & Whitney PW120 turboprops that generate an impressive 1,800 shp. This version of the ATR is configured to accommodate 44 passengers with rows of two seats on either side of a centre aisle. Inter-Canadian airliners service 19 destinations in Quebec.

(Below):
Still in the livery of Comair (the abbreviated form of South Africa's Commercial Airways), this ATR 42 was scheduled to adopt the British Airways logo starting in October 1996 under a franchise agreement with the large British airline.

(Above):
Founded in 1984, American Eagle has become one of the leading regional airlines in the United States averaging more than 10 flights a day to each of about 150 destinations. The four carriers operating under the American Eagle banner are controlled by AMR, the corporate parent of American Airlines. The American Eagle fleet is remarkably young with an average age of 4.15 years. This ATR 42 is one of 46 in the fleet.

(Below):
During the peak winter months, American Eagle ATR 42s bring tourists to the far reaches of the Florida Keys. This airliner is departing from Key West International Airport.

(Above):
The extraordinarily hectic operations at Chicago O'Hare International, the world's busiest airport, include flights of American Eagle ATR 42s.

(Below):
The weather is usually ideal for American Eagle ATR 42s operating during the peak winter months at Key West International Airport.

ATR 72

Offspring of the original ATR design includes the stretched version, the ATR 72, which entered service in 1989 and is capable of seating up to 74 passengers. This American Eagle ATR 72 (in the foreground) can be seen flying in formation with its little brother, the ATR 42.

(Above):
Illustrating the fact that commuter airliners connect spokes to hubs is this American Eagle ATR 72 taxying from a terminal at the world's busiest airport, Chicago O'Hare International.

British World Airlines operates the ATR 72, which can land in less than 4,000 feet at sea-level. This is an important advantage that turboprops possess, and which allows their use at airports which might otherwise be inaccessible to scheduled airliners. The newer ATR 72-210 has more powerful engines, generating 2,475 shp, which contribute to a take-off roll that is about 600 feet shorter at sea-level than that required for the earlier model ATR 72.

Avro Regional Jet
(British Aerospace 146)

The first BAe 146 entered service in 1983. A whole series of similarly configured aircraft evolved, including this Avro RJ 70.

(Above):
The BAe 146 was developed as the HS 146 by Hawker Siddeley, one of the precursors to British Aerospace. The first example flew in 1981. The four turbofan engines are very quiet, and thus, the aircraft quickly became popular among airlines operating at inner city airports. The model shown is flown by Eurowings.

(Below):
The high wing configuration of the Avro RJ family, unusual for a four-engine airliner, contributes to impressive field performance. This RJ 100 is operated by CityFlyer in the markings of British Airways, and has been nicknamed 'Waves of the City'.

(Opposite Above):
The RJ Series, including this RJ 85 in the colours of Azzurra Air, can be outfitted with airstairs for operations at remote airfields. These aircraft are also airbridge compatible for operations at airports with considerable infrastructure.

(Opposite Below):
Reflecting the trend of airlines away from the use of turboprops and towards the employment of jets on their regional routes is this Avro RJ in Northwest markings.

(Above):
Founded right after World War II, British World Airlines began flying a civil variant of the famed Lancaster bomber. Having come a long way from those days, the company now operates this BAe 146-300, a spacious aircraft compared to other commuter airliners. With 110 seats, this jet-powered aircraft also has a greater capacity than almost any other commuter airliner.

The logical extension of the BAe 146 Series began with the development of the Avro Regional Jet (or RJ) airliners, the first of which was the RJ70. Based on the BAe 146-100 fuselage, the RJ70 was given more modern engines that are more powerful and fuel efficient. This National Vet Systems RJ70 banks gracefully as it manoeuvres through the sky.

(Opposite Above):
Allied Signal LF507 turbofans power this Crossair RJ85 over the scenic Swiss Alps. Maximum range is 1,500 nautical miles.

(Opposite Below):
The next in the line of progression at Avro is the RJ85, a larger aircraft than the RJ70. With five-abreast seating, the capacity is 85 passengers. If six-abreast seating is installed, a total of 100 passengers may be accommodated. The distinctive contemporary markings of Crossair are unmistakable on this RJ85.

(Above):
Operated by Lufthansa CityLine, this RJ85 services various European routes. Avro boasts that its RJs have more space in their cargo holds than any other regional jets, allowing for enhanced freight revenues even if passenger load factors are only marginal.

(Opposite Below):
This RJ85 is seen cruising over a rural community on one of the many European routes serviced by Lufthansa CityLine.

A relatively recent addition to the Belgian airline, Sabena, this RJ85 is emblazoned in a fresh paint scheme.

(Above):
At the Avro factory in Woodford, England, regional jets are readied for customers worldwide. In the foreground is an RJ100, one of 12 ordered through 1995 by Crossair, the regional affiliate of Swissair. In the background are RJ85s that have been ordered by Sabena and Lufthansa CityLine. In August 1995, Sabena placed an order for 23 RJ85s which represented the largest single order for the aircraft up to that time.

(Below):
Turkish Airlines operates a fleet of 14 Avro RJs including this RJ100. The various models within the RJ family give airlines the ability to match capacity with demand. It also helps that all models, having the same basic design, share maintenance and operational commonality.

Jetstream 31 and 41

Introduced in 1982, the Jetstream 31 soon became an effective competitor in the 18-seat class. This example is operated by Air Ostrava of the Czech Republic.

In 1988, a newer variant of the Jetstream 31 was developed. Known as the Super 31, this aircraft featured more powerful engines which improved hot-and-high performance. In addition, the Super 31 offered a more spacious cabin with better noise and vibration insulation. The Super 31 gives added capability to American Eagle on its routes in the steamy and humid southern United States.

(Opposite Above):
The Jetstream 41 represented a noticeable fuselage stretch of the earlier Jetstream 31. Sixteen feet longer to accommodate up to 29 passengers, the Jetstream 41 uses the Allied Signal TRE331-14GR/HR turboprops rated at 1,500 shp. Manx Airlines operates 15 Jetstreams.

(Opposite Below):
Pictured in the livery of British Airways Express, this Manx-operated Jetstream 41 can cruise at up to 340 mph.

Beechcraft 1900C and 1900D

Gulfstream International Airlines, a relatively recent start-up based in Miami Springs, Florida, operates a fleet of Beechcraft 1900C commuter airliners. The company's growing route structure extends throughout Florida and the nearby islands.

(Below):
These nimble regional aircraft, produced by the same company that manufactures the venerable King Air corporate twin-turbo-prop, have very rapid turn-around times. This Gulfstream International Airlines Beechcraft 1900C is departing Miami International Airport after deplaning passengers and re-boarding a new set of passengers in just a matter of minutes.

(Opposite Above):
A newer version of the Beechcraft commuter airliner, the 1900D, is operated by United Express.

(Opposite Below):
A total of 255 Beechcraft 1900Cs have been delivered since the model's introduction in 1984. This Gulfstream International Airlines example is departing a southern Florida airport.

(Above):
The newer variant of the Beechcraft type, the 1900D, was introduced into commercial service in 1991. This aircraft, in Continental Express markings, was designed to enhance passenger comfort. Headroom was increased such that the aisle allows for stand-up movement. This explains the hump-like fuselage appearance.

(Opposite Above):
The Beechcraft 1900D, like this example in the colours of Air Labrador, is equipped with Pratt & Whitney PT6A-67D turboprops and an advanced flight instrumentation system.

(Opposite Below):
Skyway Airlines was launched in 1994 as Astral Aviation, a subsidiary of Midwest Express, which in turn was a unit of the brand-name tissue company, Kimberly-Clark Corporation. The airline was an outgrowth of the giant paper company's in-house corporate flight department. Skyway started operations with 12 Beechcraft 1900Ds, and now, from its hub in Milwaukee, offers service to six states in the upper Midwest and to one Canadian province.

(Above):
This USAir Express Beechcraft 1900D is seen cruising over a wide expanse of cultivated cropland. Maximum cruising speed is 320 mph and the service ceiling is 33,000 feet.

(Below):
At this angle of bank, the Beechcraft 1900D flown by USAir Express highlights the unusual control surfaces, such as the stabilons which enhance pitch stability and widen the centre of gravity range. The winglets and tailets are also clearly in view.

British Aerospace ATP

Brought to market in 1988 with high hopes, the British Aerospace Advanced Turboprop (ATP) failed to catch on. Although offering certain positive operational features, such as low-noise output, its cruise speed was not really competitive.

Canadair Regional Jet

Built by the Canadair subsidiary of Montreal-based Bombardier, the Regional Jet is an example of how commuter airlines are moving closer to resembling their big brothers at the major air carriers. Significantly higher-performing in the cruise phase of flight than turboprops, the Regional Jet can over-fly inclement weather at 41,000 feet and can attain cruise speeds of up to 530mph. Comair operates a growing fleet of these commuter airliners under the Delta Connection banner.

(Opposite Above):
The Canadair Regional Jets operated by Air Canada provide service to cross-border destinations in Canada and the United States. The aircraft seats 50 in rows of two on either side of a centre aisle.

(Opposite Below):
As more commuter airlines convert from turboprops to pure jets, they are looking for ways to distinguish themselves in the market-place. Elevating the level of service extended to the passengers is one technique. On its Canadair Regional Jets, Lufthansa's CityLine has begun to promote its City Class service, which includes a meal service comparable to that offered on major airliners, an extensive selection of newspapers and magazines, and leather-upholstered seats.

(Opposite Above):
Operating within Lufthansa's European route network, the Canadair Regional Jet has become quite popular due to the speed afforded by its two General Electric CF34 3A1 engines, each producing 9,220 lb of thrust.

(Opposite Below):
Being able to cruise above the weather is a decided advantage of the Canadair Regional Jet. This one in Lufthansa CityLine livery is seen skimming over the clouds.

(Above):
In late 1996 the Bombardier Regional Aircraft Division of Downsview, Ontario, which oversees Canadair, announced that a total of 138 Regional Jets had been delivered and another 35 were on order. This America West Express Regional Jet is representative of the type's international penetration.

(Left):
Having entered service in 1992, the Canadair Regional Jet has proven to be both cost-effective and passenger-friendly. There is six feet of headroom in the cabin and the aircraft is quiet for a jet. Including backlog, Tyrolean has orders for seven Regional Jets.

(Top):
DAC Air, the Romanian regional airline, operates a small fleet of Canadair Regional Jets. As old political divisions continue to crumble and as trade opportunities expand between the free-market nations of the West and the countries of the former Eastern Bloc, increased sales of newly-developed aerospace products like the Canadair Regional Jet to airlines like DAC Air may be expected.

(Above):
Long a manufacturer of a distinguished jet-powered corporate/executive transport called the Challenger, in the 1980s, after being acquired by Bombardier, Canadair decided to pursue the idea of 'growing' the Challenger into a 50-seat airliner. This Canadair Regional Jet is operated by Southern Winds, formerly Pampas Air.

(Above):
As numerous commuter airlines build experience on the Regional Jet, Canadair is undertaking the development of the CRJ-X, a 70-seat variant. The new aircraft will be 15.5 feet longer and the wingspan will be 12 feet wider. The aircraft will be offered in two versions, one having a 1,700 nautical mile range and the other having a 2,040 nautical mile range.

(Opposite Above):
Fresh out of the paint shop, this Mesa Airlines Regional Jet still sports a Canadian registration, reflecting the country of manufacture. Before starting scheduled service on its routes in the United States, the aircraft's registration, seen on the empennage, converted to an American registration with the standard US prefix of 'N'.

(Opposite Below):
An interesting feature of the Midway paint scheme is the repetition of the company's logo on the winglets, both outboard and inboard.

CASA C.212 and CN.235

The CASA C.212-300 has its roots in a light military transport developed for the Spanish Air Force in the early 1970s. This model, shown in the markings of Satena, can seat up to 26 passengers in rows of three-abreast. A rear cargo door can permit ready access to the fuselage.

(Opposite Above):
In collaboration with Indonesia's IPTN, CASA developed the 44-seat CN.235. It entered service in 1986. This aircraft is seen in the colours of Spain's Binter Canarias.

(Opposite Below):
The CN.235, pictured here in the livery of Binter Canarias, is powered by two General Electric CT7-9C turboprop engines. Its maximum cruise speed is 244 knots and its range is 863 nautical miles. The rear cargo door and the wide cabin have made the CN.235 appealing to military services with light airlift requirements. In fact, the aircraft has been more widely used as a military transport than as a civil airliner.

Cessna 402

(Below):
Cape Air operates a fleet of 27 Cessna 402s, piston-powered twins with seating capacity for eight passengers. Cruising speed is 174 knots.

(Bottom):
Destinations serviced by Cape Air include smaller communities along the coastal regions of Massachusetts and Florida. This Cessna 402 is departing Key West International Airport, which is located at the southern-most tip of Florida.

De Havilland Dash 7

The de Havilland Dash 7 is noted for its low noise levels. The Pratt & Whitney Canada PT6A-50 turboprop engines, producing 1,120 shp, drive sophisticated slow-turning propellers. The aircraft has been an environmental favorite at city airports. A Dash 7 in USAir Express livery is pictured in the foreground.

(Below):
The four engines of the de Havilland Dash 7 provide an extra margin of comfort for over-mountain routes, such as those operated by Tyrolean Airways. However, the Dash 7 was conceived in the era pre-dating the devastating oil embargo of 1973–74. As a four-engine turboprop, the Dash 7 is not noted for fuel economy. Only 114 Dash 7s were built.

De Havilland Dash 8

Configured for 37 passengers, this de Havilland Dash 8-100 operated by Canadian Regional Airlines serves part of the company's extensive route system throughout Canada and the United States. The company was formed in 1991 to manage the commuter air carriers of Canadian Airlines.

(Opposite):
Tyrolean Airways continues to modernise its fleet. Note the statement on the engine nacelle – 'The Sounds of Silence' – a reminder of the Dash 8's relatively quiet engines.

(Above):
Northwest Airlink, operated by Mesa Aviation, provides service in the de Havilland Dash 8-100/200. With pressurised cabin, stand-up headroom exceeding 76 inches, low noise levels, and a cruise speed of 287 knots, this aircraft has been a formidable competitor. The bright red paint scheme is very eye-catching.

(Below):
De Havilland of Canada is now owned by Bombardier, a Canadian company founded in 1942 as a manufacturer of snowmobiles. In addition to de Havilland, the Bombardier aerospace group is comprised of Canadair, Learjet, and Shorts. For a short time de Havilland was owned by Boeing. The ruggedness of the Dash 8 airframes is expected to give the aircraft a useful commercial airline lifetime of 32 years. This is a Dash 8-100 flown by Tyrolean Airways.

(Left):
Shown taxying at Toronto City Centre Airport, this Dash 8-100 in Air Ontario livery is nearly dwarfed by the shining lights of the night skyline of Toronto. Formed in 1987 through a merger of two Canadian airline companies, Air Ontario operates an all-Dash 8 fleet.

De Havilland added to its high-wing, T-tail line with the introduction into commercial service of the twin-engine Dash 8 in 1984. This family of regional transports has grown to include the Series 100/200 with seating for 37 to 39, the Series 300 with seating for 50 to 56, and the Series 400 with seating for 70 to 78. Interestingly, the newer Dash 8-types, though twin-engined, have greater seating capacity than the older four-engined Dash 7, which could accommodate 46 to 50 passengers. Pictured here is a Dash 8-300 in the colours of USAir Express.

The distinctive tent-like roofing of the new Denver International Airport serves as a fitting backdrop for this Dash 8-100 which is operated by United Express. Denver is a major hub for United Air Lines.

Reflecting its military lineage, the Dash 8 has large, wide-span slotted flaps that allow for good short-field performance.

Dash 8 Series aircraft, like this DAC Air Series 300, are expected to last 80,000 flight hours and 60,000 take-off and landing cycles.

British Airways Express operates the Dash 8-300 at Bristol Airport. All Dash 8 models employ a noise and vibration suppression system that reduces noise and vibration through active absorption so that levels are similar to some jet-powered airliners.

(Opposite Above):
The largest regional air carrier in Canada, Canadian Regional Airlines operates 14 Dash 8-300s as part of an overall fleet of 54 aircraft. Based in Calgary, the company has many destinations in western Canada.

(Opposite Below):
The Dash 8's main landing gear struts, which are quite substantial, fold up into the engine nacelles.

Brymon Airways operates this Dash 8-300 in the colours of British Airways, which acquired the company in 1993. The airline, whose name derives from a combining of the names of its two founders, Bill Bryce and Chris Amon, has long used de Havilland aircraft. In fact, Brymon Airways was the first British airline to employ the Dash 8.

(Opposite):
The de Havilland family of twin turboprops is firmly established in the commuter airliner marketplace. This is a Dash 8-100.

Dornier Do 228 and Do 328

Conceived in the early 1980s, the Dornier Do 228 has met with market success, a total of 230 having been delivered worldwide. The Do 228 is considered a workhorse among 19-seat commuter airliners. It has good short-field capabilities and, according to the manufacturer, better single-engine performance than all competing aircraft in the same class. Reflecting the aircraft's penetration of the global market-place, this Do 228 is operated by Taiwan Airways.

(Left):
The launch customer for the Dornier Do 328 was the Swiss regional carrier Air Engiadina, which took delivery of its first such aircraft in 1993. This aircraft can seat 31 and cruise at 335 knots.

(Below):
Because of the speed obtainable by the Do 328, seen here in Air Engiadina markings, along with its typical route of a few hundred miles, actual elapsed time on such routes is highly competitive with jetliners.

In August 1994, the Nigerian airline Afrimex Aviation took delivery of its first Do 328. Operating reliability is extremely important considering the remoteness of the airline's destinations.

(Opposite Above):
Formosa Airlines is among the growing list of operators of the Dornier Do 328. This version of the aircraft is configured for 33 passengers.

(Opposite Below):
The Do 328 can fly at altitudes of up to 31,000 feet and can cover distances of up to 1,000 nautical miles with a full passenger load. Seating is three-abreast with an off-centre aisle.

Being a fairly new design, the Dornier Do 328 features an advanced technology cockpit. The Honeywell Primus 2000 with fully integrated avionics is standard, and includes a five-tube Electronic Flight Instrument System (EFIS). Available as an option is the Hughes/Flight Dynamics Head-Up Guidance System (HGS), which displays vital flight data on a glass screen within the pilot's field of view to permit landings in low visibility situations. This Do 328 belongs to Lone Star Airlines.

(Opposite Above):
Thailand's PB Air is among the many world-wide operators of the Dornier Do 328.

(Opposite Below):
As has become common with the more established manufacturers of commuter airliners, optional offerings are available to purchasers so that their aircraft may be tailored to specific needs. For example, Dornier makes the Do 328 available in different seating configurations – from 30 seats to 39 seats. Also, 'hot-and-high' power-plants are options for airlines operating out of mountainous or desert locations. This Do 328 is in the colours of Air France/Air Inter.

(Above):
Air Stord is a commuter airline operating the Dornier Do 328 in Norway. Because of the Do 328's high cruise speed, air traffic control can sequence the aircraft in line with jetliners at major hubs, avoiding a slow-down in air traffic flow.

(Below):
Commuter airlines are trying to improve the level of comfort offered to passengers. Accordingly, regional aircraft manufacturers are working with component suppliers to, among other things, reduce interior noise levels. The Do 328, like this example in Mountain Air Express markings, has low rpm in cruise engines and six-blade composite propellers that tend to lessen noise output.

EMBRAER EMB-120 Brasilia

Founded by the Brazilian government in 1969, Empresa Brasileira de Aeronautica S.A. (EMBRAER) was privatised in 1994. Its Brasilia aircraft was an outgrowth of the earlier Bandeirante commuter airliner.

The Brasilia has been a popular choice among regional airlines with over 300 having been ordered by companies in 14 countries. Cincinnati-based Comair operates 40 EMB-120s.

The EMBRAER EMB-120 Brasilia can be configured for as many as 30 passengers. Comair, which operates a Delta Connection service, is among the larger regional airlines in the United States with an extensive route system in the south-eastern and mid-western parts of the country.

(Opposite Above):
The Brasilia first entered commercial airline service in 1985. Among the many operators of the EMB-120 is USAir Express.

(Opposite Below):
The EMB-120 has a pressurised cabin, colour weather radar, and accommodations for a full service galley. Ramp self-sufficiency and quick turn-around time make the Brasilia attractive to regional air carriers like Continental Express.

Inter Brasil operates the indigenous commuter airliner. High-tech products like the Brasilia can be a source of pride for a country as well as a meaningful contributor to foreign export revenues.

Fairchild Metro 23

In the 1960s, Swearingen Aviation developed the predecessor to what is now known as the Metro 23. Fairchild Industries, now Fairchild Aircraft Incorporated, acquired the company in 1971, and the Swearingen name was discontinued. A family of ever larger and more powerful twin-turboprops called Merlins and Metros proceeded to emerge from the Texas factory. More than 1,000 models of these aircraft have been delivered to 84 airlines. This Metro 23 is in the colours of China Hainan Airlines.

(Below): Kendell Airlines is among the many regional air carriers in the US operating the Metro 23. The aircraft is powered by Allied Signal TPE331-12UAR turboprop engines generating 1,000 shp. The aircraft's slender fuselage and streamlined features contribute to the maximum cruise speed of 291 knots. The elongated nose is used for storing passenger baggage. There is two-abreast seating for a total of 19 passengers.

Fokker F27

Associated with the lithe fighter flown in heralded World War I air battles by the Red Baron, Fokker is one of the grand old names in aviation. Competitive pressures finally caught up with the company, and after a long successful run, it, like von Richthofen, perished with a glorious legacy. Without an infusion of financing or a merger partner stepping forward, the Fokker company simply faded from the scene. However, its many contributions to the commuter airline world will live on for years to come. The F27 Friendship is a design that dates back to the 1950s when air carriers were looking for turboprops to replace radial-engined airliners. Of the 786 Friendships built in all versions, 205 were constructed by Fairchild in the US. This is an F27 in Air UK colours.

(Below):
Despite the age of the Fokker F27, several hundred continue to be in operation today. The longevity of this design is a tribute to the design's underlying logic and to the ruggedness of the aircraft's construction. Comair, South Africa's largest privately owned airline, founded in 1946, operates four 40-seat Friendships.

Fokker 50

Obviously, a follow-on to its very popular
F27, the Fokker 50 entered commercial
airline service in 1987 as a larger and
advanced version of the earlier Friendship.
This Fokker 50 belongs to TAM of Brazil.

The operating characteristics and configuration of the Fokker 50 made it adaptable to uses other than commuter airline service. For example, versions were offered for carrying freight and for maritime patrol.

This Fokker 50 in Air UK colours is virtually indistinguishable in terms of markings from the same airline's F27. The similarity of types within the aircraft family as well as the longevity of the different models attests to the basic integrity of the original design.

The designation of the Fokker 50 derived from the number of passengers it can seat. The standard Fokker 50 comes equipped with two Pratt & Whitney Canada PW125B turboprops rated at 2,500 shp. A hot-and-high variant of the aircraft was available with higher-rated power-plants. This Fokker 50 is flown by Philippine Airlines.

(Opposite Above):
Aer Lingus Commuter, based at Dublin Airport in Ireland, operates six Fokker 50s among other aircraft. The airline services more than one million passengers annually.

(Opposite Below):
A mark of a good commercial aircraft is its use in the far corners of the world. The Fokker family of commuter airliners has been well-received globally. This Fokker 50 servicing passengers in Ethiopia is a good example.

Well over 225 Fokker 50s were delivered,
and like the earlier F27s, they have become
workhorses for commuter air carriers like
Royal Brunei.

Varig Brazilian Airlines operates Rio-Sul, a regional air carrier with a hub at Rio de Janeiro. The Rio-Sul fleet includes the Fokker 50.

(Above):
KLM CityHopper provides service to 30 destinations in 12 countries. It operates 10 Fokker 50s. The airline is, of course, partial to the Fokker brand since both KLM and Fokker share Dutch roots.

(Below):
Seating arrangement for the Fokker 50 is four-abreast with a centre aisle. The long list of commuter air carriers operating the Fokker 50 includes Formosa Airlines.

Fokker F28

Canadian Regional Airlines operates the early-model Fokker F28 Fellowship, the inevitable jet-powered addition to Fokker's product line following the popularity of the F27. The aircraft is powered by two Rolls-Royce Spey engines. Developed in the 1960s, this version of the Fellowship can seat 65 passengers. Later models of the F28 were stretched to accommodate more passengers. A total of 248 F28s were delivered.

Fokker 70

Developed by Fokker in the early 1990s to complement the company's smaller F28 and large Fokker 100, the Fokker 70 can seat 79 passengers.

(Opposite Above):
British Midland was among the early customers for the Fokker 70. The two Rolls-Royce Tay turbofans each produce up to 13,850 lb of thrust.

(Opposite Below):
The first US customer for the Fokker 70 was America West Express, which took delivery on 12 June 1995.

Hungary's regional air service needs are satisfied in part by this Malev Fokker 70.

(Opposite Above):
The Fokker 70, like this example in Vietnam Airlines livery, can cruise at an altitude of up to 35,000 feet and at a maximum speed of 462 knots.

(Opposite Below):
Avianova, based in Rome, operates eight Fokker 70s.

Different models of the Fokker 70 include a 70-seat version (versus the 79-seat version) albeit with greater cargo capacity, an ER or extended range version, and a corporate shuttle version. This Fokker 70 is operated by Austrian Airlines.

Fokker 100

(Above):
With a range of 1,680 nautical miles and a standard seating capacity of 107 passengers, the Fokker 100 did not exactly fit the definition of a commuter airliner when entering commercial service in 1988. Yet, with commuter airliners being designed in the 1990s with jet engines, longer operating radii, and bigger cabins, perhaps the Fokker 100 was just a little ahead of its time. US Airways operates this example of the Fokker 100.

(Below):
Conceived as a stretched and upgraded version of the F28, the Fokker 100 was part of a bold plan to introduce at the same time both a new jetliner and a new turboprop, the Fokker 50. American Airlines, one of the largest US air carriers, owns 71 Fokker 100s.

(Above):
Before the manufacturer fell on hard times, there was an ambitious plan to produce a Fokker 130, an elongated version of the Fokker 100 that could accommodate from 116 to 137 passengers. This Fokker 100 is in the colours of British Midland.

(Below):
Because of its larger seating capacity, the Fokker 100 has to have two over-wing emergency exit doors on each side of the fuselage.

(Above):
The worldwide acceptance of Fokker's biggest jet airliner is evidenced by the large number of airlines across the globe operating the type. This is a Fokker 100 in the colours of Formosa Airlines.

(Below):
David Hinson, former Administrator of the Federal Aviation Administration, is an experienced airline pilot and a founder of Midway Airlines. Although the airline ceased operations, it was later resurrected.

Before the manufacturer fell on hard times, there was an ambitious plan to produce a Fokker 130, an elongated version of the Fokker 100 that could accommodate from 116 to 137 passengers. This Fokker 100 is in the colours of Iran Air.

(Opposite Above):
Korean Air Lines operates 13 Fokker 100s.
Many versions of the Fokker 100 are
equipped with the Rolls-Royce Tay 650
turbofan engines rated at 15,100 lb of thrust.

(Opposite Below):
The first model of the Fokker 100 was
outfitted with Rolls-Royce Tay 620 turbofans producing 13,850 lb of thrust. Seen here
is a Fokker 100 in the colours of Portugalia.

Seen here in Air Ivoire livery, the Fokker 100 has an advanced flight instrumentation system that includes six colour displays, weather radar, and ARINC 700 avionics.

(Opposite Above):
The seating configuration for the Fokker 100 is five-abreast with an off-centre aisle. There are typically two galleys to serve the more than one hundred passengers. This Fokker 100 is in Transwede colours.

(Opposite Below):
Stansted-based Air UK has a fleet that includes 11 Fokker 100s. The airline has more than 73,000 flight departures annually that carry over 3.3 million passengers.

One of the larger air carriers in the world, KLM Royal Dutch Airlines operates a massive and diverse fleet that includes six Fokker 100s.

Grumman Turbo Mallard

(Below):
Although hardly comparable to the sumptuous clippers of the late 1930s, this Grumman amphibian in Pan American markings rekindles memories of a more glamorous time in commercial air travel. Known as the Pan Am Air Bridge, this small airline has ties to a resurrected Pan Am that is trying to restore the good name of the former premier flag carrier of the US. An investor group bought the rights to the famous name in the wake of the original Pan Am's demise, and established an Airbus A300 service between New York and Miami as well as between New York and San Juan. An affiliate operates Grumman Mallards with turboprop conversions, like the one seen here, from Miami's Watson Island Seaplane Base to some of the nearby islands.

(Bottom):
A charming relic of a bygone era, the Grumman Mallard was operated on south Florida routes for many years by Chalk's Flying Service. The landing gear is folded up as the aircraft taxies out and its weight is displaced in the waters next to the Watson Island Seaplane Base. Some of Miami's skyscrapers are visible in the distance. Passengers are treated to an old-time flying adventure aboard the Pan Am Air Bridge.

Saab 340

(Above):
The Saab 340 has emerged as a major player in the 35-seat commuter airliner class, with American Eagle among its many operators. Originated by a joint venture of Saab and Fairchild in 1980, this type's production was eventually taken over by Saab alone as Fairchild ran into financial difficulties.

(Right):
First delivery of the Saab 340 occurred in 1984 to the Swiss regional air carrier Crossair. Many other commuter airlines have gone on to operate the aircraft, including Air Baltic.

An upgraded version, designated the Saab 340B, was introduced in 1987. This model features the General Electric CT7-9B turboprops, rated up to 11,750 shp. Here two Saab 340Bs in American Eagle colours fly in formation. American Eagle placed a one-time order for 100 of these aircraft.

Based in Minneapolis, Mesaba Aviation is affiliated with air carrier giant Northwest Airlines as a Northwest Airlink company. The parent airline's colours are used on the commuter aircraft like this Saab 340. Northwest's hubs are at Minneapolis/St Paul, Detroit, and Memphis.

(Opposite Above):
Express Airlines is a Northwest Airlink company, flying the Saab 340.

(Opposite Below):
Posed against the trademark Chicago skyline, this Saab 340 belonging to Midway-based Chicago Express Airlines cruises over Lake Michigan. Note the silhouette of the Chicago skyline reproduced on the aircraft's vertical stabiliser and rudder.

Regional Airlines, a French commuter airline started in the early 1990s, operates the Saab 340B. The airline, which has grown rapidly, services 17 French cities and 10 European capitals.

(Opposite Above):
A common sight in US airspace is the logo of American Eagle. Note, on the tail, the ending letters in this aircraft's registration – 'AE'. The Federal Aviation Administration-issued registration reflects the government's compliance with the airline's request for initials matching its name.

(Opposite Below):
Crossair, as the launch customer for the Saab 340, has operated the aircraft longer than any other airline. This example is painted in a special, eye-catching scheme.

(Overleaf):
The standard Crossair livery blends with the snow-capped mountains as this Saab 340 skims over the Swiss Alps.

The Air Ostrava fleet includes two Saab 340s. Established in 1994 through the privatisation of the Czech Republic's state-run air operations, Air Ostrava is broadening its service both domestically and to major European centres.

Saab 2000

(Below):
Crossair was the launch customer for the Saab 2000, just as it was for the earlier Saab 340. In 1994, Crossair took delivery of its first Saab 2000. The aircraft is an elongated and far more sophisticated version of the Saab 340. The newer aircraft can accommodate from 50 to 58 passengers.

(Bottom):
Another stunning Crossair paint scheme – this one promoting the musical *Phantom of the Opera.* In addition to serving as a mobile billboard, the Saab 2000 can cruise at 31,000 feet and achieve a maximum cruise speed of 365 knots. The manufacturer boasts that the Saab 2000 offers jet-like speed and turbo-prop economy.

(Left):
Deutsche BA was created in 1992 when a consortium of three German banks and British Airways acquired an existing air-line. With hubs at Berlin and Munich, the air carrier operates more than 900 flights a week. A total of 23 destinations in eight European countries are served. Among the fleet of 21 aircraft are five Saab 2000s.

(Opposite Above):
The evolution of the Saab 2000 can be easily ascertained when viewed in proximity to the Saab 340, like this example in the livery of American Eagle.

(Opposite Below):
Crossair has given the name Concordino to the Saab 2000.

(Below):
Regional Airlines, which operates the Saab 340B, also began operating the Saab 2000. This one is configured for 53 passengers. The cockpit is outfitted with the Rockwell Collins Pro Line 4 system. There are six CRT displays.

Shorts 360

Possessing an ungainly shape, the Shorts 360 is an ageing commuter airliner still seen in service at some airports. Gulfstream International Airlines operates the type on routes connecting southern Florida with The Bahamas. This example is decorated in colours promoting the offshore resort of Sandals.

(Below):
Sporting a more conventional paint scheme for Gulfstream International Airlines, this Shorts 360 is seen operating from Key West International Airport, the southern-most airport in the US and a major stopping-off point for flights to island destinations. The boxy Shorts 360 can carry 39 passengers and cruise at 244 mph.